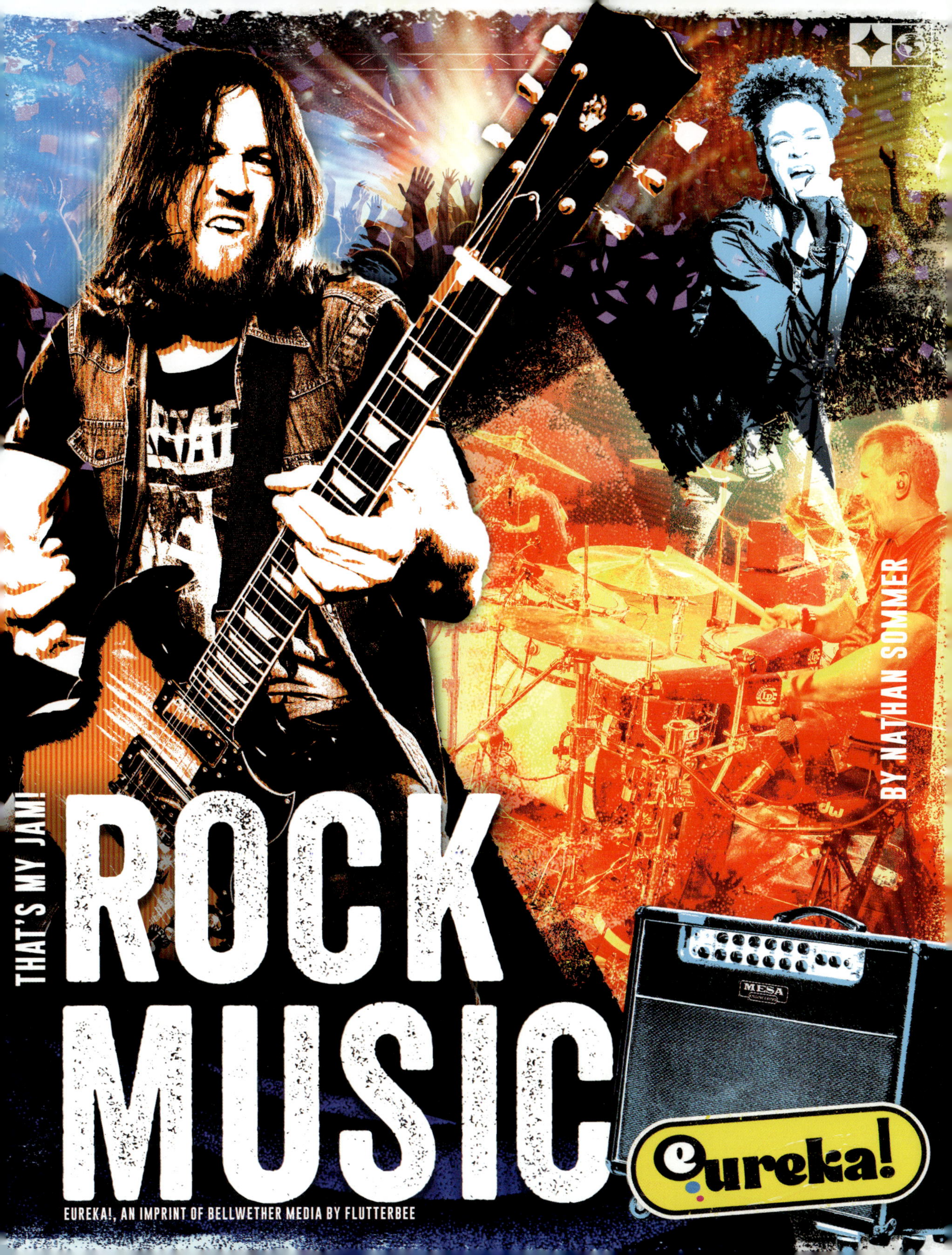

THAT'S MY JAM!

ROCK MUSIC

BY NATHAN SOMMER

eureka!

EUREKA!, AN IMPRINT OF BELLWETHER MEDIA BY FLUTTERBEE

Eureka! books turn real stories into unforgettable experiences. Clear, direct language and sharp, captivating imagery make it easy to follow your curiosity, one fascinating fact at a time.
Your Eureka! moment awaits!

This edition first published in 2027 by Bellwether Media, Inc.

For information regarding permission, write to Bellwether Media, Inc., Attention: Permissions Department, 3500 American Blvd W, Suite 150, Bloomington, MN 55431.

Names: Sommer, Nathan author
Title: Rock music / Nathan Sommer.
Description: Eureka. | Minneapolis : Bellwether Media, Inc, 2027. | Series: That's my jam! | Includes index. | Audience: Ages 9-13 | Audience: Grades 7-9 | Summary: ""Engaging images accompany information on rock music. The text level and subject matter are intended for students in grades 5 through 9"-Provided by publisher" -- Provided by publisher.
Identifiers: LCCN 2026010708 (print) | LCCN 2026010709 (ebook) | ISBN 9798898801281 (library binding) | ISBN 9798898802523 (ebook)
Subjects: LCSH: Rock music--History and criticism
Classification: LCC ML3534 .S596 2027 (print) | LCC ML3534 (ebook) | DDC 782.42166--dc23/eng/20260318

LC record available at https://lccn.loc.gov/2026010708
LC ebook record available at https://lccn.loc.gov/2026010709

Editor: Elizabeth Neuenfeldt Designer: Josh Brink

Printed in the United States of America, North Mankato, MN.

TABLE OF CONTENTS

WHAT IS ROCK?

BLACK LABEL SOCIETY

Rock is short for "rock and roll." This genre blends loud and energetic beats with powerful rhythms and melodies. Its songs heavily use guitars and drums. Rock music is known for its bold attitude. Its artists often sing about personal freedom and life's struggles. Many challenge society's norms.

MAROON 5

BEHIND THE NAME

The term "rock and roll" has been used since the 1920s. It was first included in Trixie Smith's 1922 song "My Man Rocks Me (With One Steady Roll)."

COLDPLAY

GARY CLARK JR.

Hard rock and heavy metal are well-known rock subgenres. Punk rock and grunge are also popular. Coldplay and Maroon 5 are some of rock's biggest stars today.

THE HISTORY OF ROCK

Rock music came from R & B, jazz, and country. Many believe modern rock began in the United States in the 1950s. Early rock artists included Fats Domino, Little Richard, Chuck Berry, and Elvis Presley. Rock quickly became popular with young listeners.

A YOUNG AUDIENCE

Teens in the 1950s had more money and free time than earlier generations. Rock music helped drive this new youth culture.

THE ROLLING STONES

Rock music spread overseas in the 1960s. This led to the British Invasion that gave the Beatles and the Rolling Stones major success. Hard rock bands such as Led Zeppelin and the Runaways took over in the 1970s. KISS and Queen showcased flashy looks and high-energy songs. They turned rock into performance art.

KISS

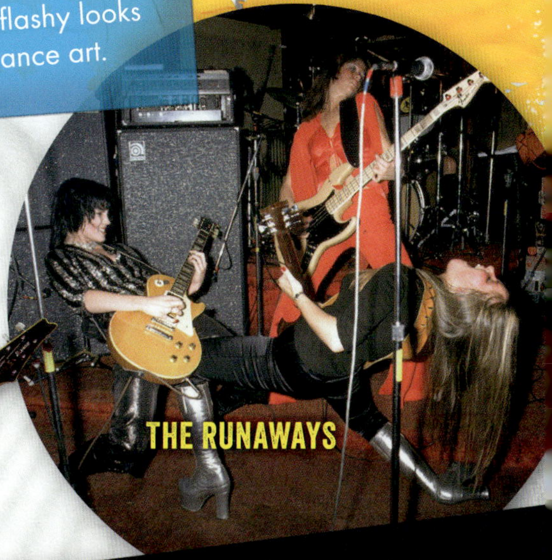

THE RUNAWAYS

LED ZEPPELIN

GREEN DAY

NIRVANA

Stadium-ready hits from Journey and Guns N' Roses ruled 1980s rock. Metallica helped heavy metal explode in popularity. Alternative rock such as grunge and punk became mainstream in the 1990s. This made superstars out of bands such as Nirvana and Green Day.

METALLICA

FALL OUT BOY

Rock branched out in new directions during the 2000s. Linkin Park famously blended rock with hip-hop. Pop-punk bands paired raw lyrics with catchy melodies. This earned bands such as blink-182 and Fall Out Boy millions of fans. Rock continued to receive major airplay during the 2000s and 2010s. Paramore and Florence and the Machine were some of the top artists.

MTV AND ROCK

MTV began in 1981. The channel made music videos an important part of every rock artist's success. It helped make bands such as Bon Jovi and Def Leppard hugely popular.

PARAMORE

LINKIN PARK

ROCK TIMELINE

1922
Trixie Smith uses the phrase "rock and roll" in her song "My Man Rocks Me (With One Steady Roll)"

1931
George Beauchamp and Adolph Rickenbacker invent the electric guitar

1956
Elvis Presley's performance on *The Ed Sullivan Show* draws around 60 million viewers

ELVIS PRESLEY

1962
The first rock award at the Grammys is presented

1964
The British Invasion comes to the U.S., leading to the rise of the Beatles and the Rolling Stones

THE BEATLES

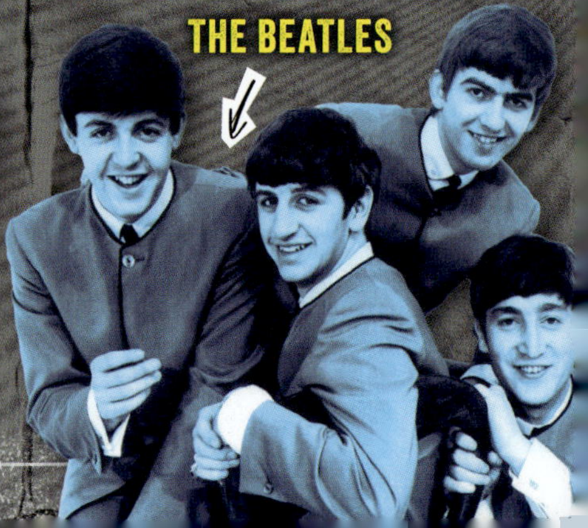

1980
AC/DC release *Back in Black*, the best-selling rock album in history

1983

The Rock & Roll Hall of Fame is formed

1985

Queen give one of history's most famous performances at Live Aid

2006

U2 win their 22nd Grammy award, a rock record

2026

Coldplay's Music of the Spheres World Tour becomes the best-selling tour in rock history

INSTRUMENTS

ELECTRIC GUITAR

George Beauchamp and Adolph Rickenbacker invented the modern electric guitar in 1931. Blues and country artists were the first to use it.

GRETA VAN FLEET

THE FIRST ELECTRIC GUITAR

Beauchamp and Rickenbacker's invention was called the Rickenbacker Electro A-22. It had a long neck and rounded shape. It was nicknamed the "Frying Pan."

DRUM KITS

Drum kits are a group of percussion instruments played by one drummer. They give rock songs their beat and tempo. Jazz artist Edward "Dee Dee" Chandler built the first modern drum kit in the 1890s.

BASS GUITAR

Bass guitars team with drum kits to give rock songs rhythm. They make deeper and lower sounds than electric guitars. Paul Tutmarc invented the first model in the mid 1930s.

AWARDS AND HONORS

GRAMMY AWARDS

The Grammys were first held in 1959. They allow musicians to choose the year's best artists and albums. The first rock Grammy was given in 1962. Top awards include Best Rock Song and Best Metal Performance.

BLACK SABBATH

THE MOST GRAMMYS

U2 have won more Grammys than any band in history. They have earned 22 Grammys as of 2026.

LINKIN PARK

BILLBOARD MUSIC AWARDS

The first *Billboard* Music Awards were held in 1990. They honor artists based on sales and radio airplay. Rock awards include Top Rock Duo/Group and Top Hard Rock Song.

ROCK & ROLL HALL OF FAME

The Rock & Roll Hall of Fame formed in 1983. It celebrates artists who have helped shape rock's history. More than 400 artists have been added so far.

ROY ORBISON AND BRUCE SPRINGSTEEN

TYPES OF ROCK

ELVIS PRESLEY

ROCK AND ROLL

Date Started: 1950s

Song: "Hound Dog" by Elvis Presley

Traits:
- inspired by blues, gospel, and country
- strong, danceable beats
- simple, catchy lyrics

HARD ROCK

Date Started: 1960s

Song: "Born to be Wild" by Steppenwolf

Traits:
- loud, energetic sound
- heavy use of electric guitars
- powerful rhythms and vocals

STEPPENWOLF

HEAVY METAL

Date Started: early 1970s

Traits:
- very loud songs
- dark themes and costumes
- heavy-hitting drum beats

Song: "Enter Sandman" by Metallica

METALLICA

SUZI QUATRO

GLAM ROCK

Date Started: early 1970s

Traits:
- blends pop with hard rock
- flashy makeup and costumes
- theatrical performances

Song: "Devil Gate Drive" by Suzi Quatro

GRUNGE

Date Started: mid 1980s

Traits:

- blends punk rock with heavy metal
- heavily distorted guitars
- dark lyrics

Song: "All Apologies" by Nirvana

NIRVANA

ARENA ROCK

Date Started: mid 1970s

Traits:

- music made for large audiences
- powerful and memorable choruses
- frequent guitar solos

Song: "Don't Stop Believin'" by Journey

JOURNEY

PUNK ROCK

Date Started: mid 1970s

Traits:
- short songs with fast tempos
- raw and often shouted vocals
- lyrics about social and political issues

Song:

"Bad Reputation" by Joan Jett & the Blackhearts

JOAN JETT & THE BLACKHEARTS

FALL OUT BOY

EMO ROCK

Date Started: mid 1980s

Traits:
- mix of punk, hard rock, and pop
- catchy melodies
- emotional lyrics

Song:

"Sugar, We're Goin Down" by Fall Out Boy

ROCK PROFILES

CHUCK BERRY

Chuck Berry is called the Father of Rock and Roll. He helped create rock and roll from R & B.

GETTING STARTED

Berry started performing music in high school. He soon learned to play guitar. He joined the Sir John Trio in 1953. Two years later, he recorded his first song, "Maybellene." It was on the pop charts for 11 weeks!

Birthday:
October 18, 1926

Death:
March 18, 2017

Hometown:
St. Louis, Missouri

Types of Music:
rock and roll, R & B, country

First Hit Song:
"Maybellene"
(1955)

HIT RELEASES

- *After School Session* (1957)
- *Berry Is On Top* (1959)
- *New Juke Box Hits* (1961)
- *Fresh Berry's* (1965)
- *Chuck* (2017)

HIT SONG MAKER

Berry kept making hit songs. "Johnny B. Goode" helped define rock and roll. "Roll Over, Beethoven!" and "Memphis" were also popular songs.

BREAKING BARRIERS

Berry helped make a new type of music. His work broke barriers for Black artists.

TIMELINE

1952
Berry starts playing guitar in a band

1953
Berry joins the Sir John Trio, which is later renamed the Chuck Berry Combo

1955
Berry records "Maybellene," his first hit song

1986
Berry is added to the Rock & Roll Hall of Fame

2017
Berry passes away

ELVIS PRESLEY

Elvis Presley is called the King of Rock and Roll. He is one of music's most recognizable figures.

A MOST-WATCHED ARTIST

In 1953, Presley paid to record a song for his mother. He was discovered at the studio. His early television performances broke viewership records.

Birthday:
January 8, 1935

Death:
August 16, 1977

Hometown:
Tupelo, Mississippi

Types of Music:
rock and roll, R & B, country

First Hit Song:
"That's All Right" (1954)

TIMELINE

1953
Presley is discovered at a recording studio in Memphis, Tennessee

1954
"That's All Right" becomes Presley's first hit in the U.S.

1956
"Heartbreak Hotel" sells more than one million copies

FROM MUSIC TO FILM

Presley's 1956 song "Heartbreak Hotel" sold more than one million copies. He starred in the movie *Love Me Tender* the same year. He acted in over 30 movies total. He won the Grammy Lifetime Achievement Award in 1971.

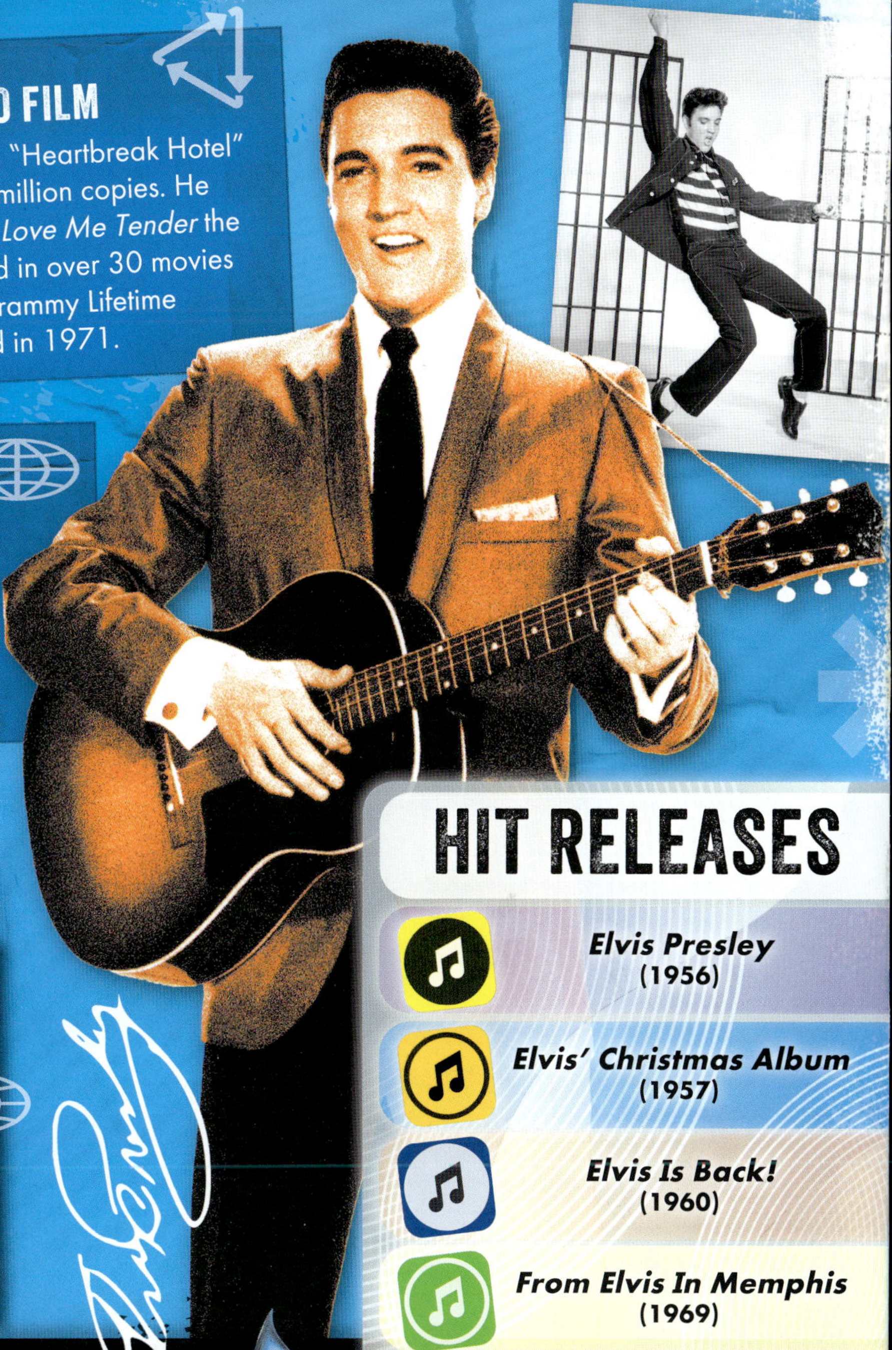

RECORD SALES

Presley's one billion records sold are more than any artist in history. He had seven songs top the *Billboard* Hot 100.

GRACELAND

Presley's home in Memphis, Tennessee, is called Graceland. It is one of the most-visited homes in the U.S.

HIT RELEASES

- ***Elvis Presley*** **(1956)**
- ***Elvis' Christmas Album*** **(1957)**
- ***Elvis Is Back!*** **(1960)**
- ***From Elvis In Memphis*** **(1969)**
- ***Aloha from Hawaii Via Satellite*** **(1973)**

1969

"Suspicious Minds" becomes Presley's seventh song to top the *Billboard* Hot 100

1971

Presley wins the Grammy Lifetime Achievement Award

THE BEATLES

The Beatles are music's best-selling band. Their worldwide success changed rock forever.

BEATLEMANIA

The Beatles began playing together in 1962. "Love Me Do" was an instant hit that year. Their music became popular worldwide. This was known as "Beatlemania."

NUMBER ONE ALBUMS

In 1964, *Meet the Beatles!* became their first chart-topping album. They had 19 number one albums total. The 1967 album *Sgt. Pepper's Lonely Hearts Club Band* is often called the most important rock album ever.

BILLBOARD HISTORY

In 1964, the Beatles earned all top five spots on the *Billboard* Hot 100. They were the first artists to do so.

Notable Members:
Paul McCartney, John Lennon, George Harrison, Ringo Starr

Place Formed:
Liverpool, England

Dates Active:
1962–1970

Types of Music:
pop rock, folk

First Hit Song:
"Love Me Do" (1962)

THE BEATLES

HIT RELEASES

- *A Hard Day's Night* (1964)
- *Revolver* (1966)
- *Sgt. Pepper's Lonely Hearts Club Band* (1967)
- *Abbey Road* (1969)
- *Let It Be* (1970)

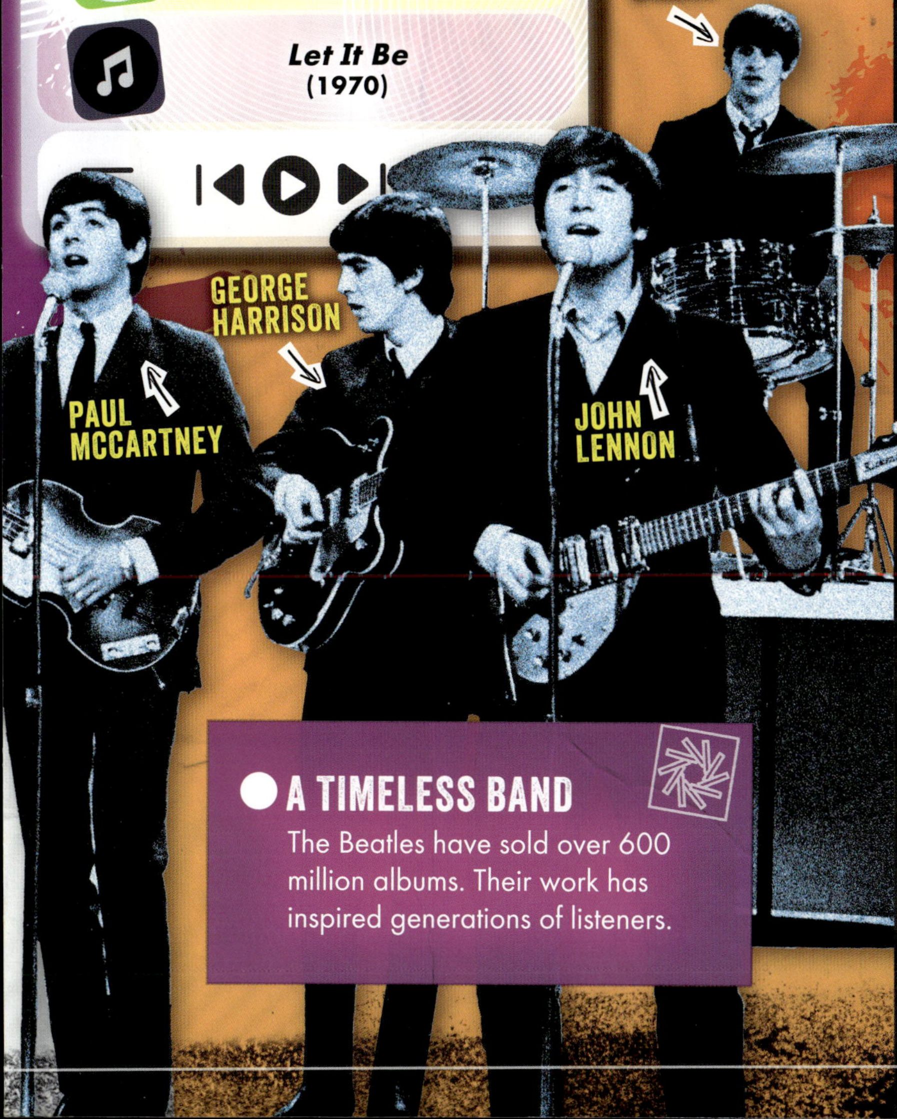

A TIMELESS BAND

The Beatles have sold over 600 million albums. Their work has inspired generations of listeners.

TIMELINE

1957
Paul McCartney, John Lennon, and George Harrison begin making music together

1962
Ringo Starr joins the band and "Love Me Do" becomes the Beatles's first major hit

1964
The Beatles lead the British Invasion in the U.S., scoring their first number one album

1967
Sgt. Pepper's Lonely Hearts Club Band is released

1970
The Beatles earn their record-breaking 20th *Billboard* number one song

THE ROLLING STONES

The Rolling Stones are one of rock's longest-running acts. They are nicknamed the World's Greatest Rock and Roll Band.

BLUES BEGINNINGS

The Rolling Stones formed in 1962. They performed blues rock in London clubs. In 1965, "(I Can't Get No) Satisfaction" topped charts worldwide.

GRAMMY WINNERS

They released their first original album, *Aftermath*, in 1966. Their 2023 album *Hackney Diamonds* later won the Grammy for Best Rock Album.

TIMELINE

1962
The Rolling Stones form in London

1965
"(I Can't Get No) Satisfaction" becomes the Rolling Stones's first chart-topping hit worldwide

1966
The Rolling Stones first original album, *Aftermath*, is released

Notable Members:
Mick Jagger, Keith Richards, Ronnie Wood, Charlie Watts, Bill Wyman

Place Formed:
London, England

Dates Active:
1962–present

Types of Music:
blues rock, hard rock, pop rock

First Hit Song:
"Come On" (1963)

DECADES OF SUCCESS

The Rolling Stones scored a *Billboard* top 10 album seven decades in a row. They are the first band to do this. They were added to the Rock & Roll Hall of Fame in 1989.

1989
The Rolling Stones are added to the Rock & Roll Hall of Fame

2025
Hackney Diamonds earns the group their fourth Grammy win

HIT RELEASES

- ***Beggars Banquet*** (1968)
- ***Let It Bleed*** (1969)
- ***Sticky Fingers*** (1971)
- ***Some Girls*** (1978)
- ***Tattoo You*** (1981)

JIMI HENDRIX

Jimi Hendrix was a skilled guitarist. He is said to be the most gifted instrumentalist of all time.

HIT RELEASES

Are You Experienced **(1967)**

Axis: Bold as Love **(1967)**

Electric Ladyland **(1968)**

The Cry of Love **(1971)**

THE JIMI HENDRIX EXPERIENCE

Hendrix first played for other musicians. In 1966, he formed the band the Jimi Hendrix Experience. Their first hit was "Hey Joe." Their first album, *Are You Experienced*, reached number five on the *Billboard* Hot 200.

WOODSTOCK

Jimi Hendrix performed at Woodstock Music & Art Fair in 1969. He played his own version of "Star Spangled Banner." It was unforgettable!

TIMELINE

1966
Hendrix forms the Jimi Hendrix Experience

1967
The Jimi Hendrix experience release *Are You Experienced*

1969
Hendrix performs at Woodstock Music & Art Fair

ROCK & ROLL HALL OF FAME

Hendrix is remembered for his show-stopping guitar skills. The Jimi Hendrix Experience are added to the Rock & Roll Hall of Fame in 1992.

LEFT-HANDED

Hendrix played the guitar with his left hand. Most guitarists play with their right hand.

Birthday:
November 27, 1942

Death:
September 18, 1970

Hometown:
Seattle, Washington

Types of Music:
R & B, hard rock

First Hit Song:
"Hey Joe" (1966)

1972
Hendrix passes away

1992
The Jimi Hendrix Experience are added to the Rock & Roll Hall of Fame

FLEETWOOD MAC

Fleetwood Mac famously blended rock with pop. The band members are viewed as some of rock's greatest songwriters.

MOVING STATESIDE

Fleetwood Mac began as a British blues band in 1967. They moved to the U.S. in 1974. They soon recorded the major hits "Rhiannon" and "Landslide."

SOLO SUCCESS

Many Fleetwood Mac members had successful solo careers. Stevie Nicks is the first woman to be added to the Rock & Roll Hall of Fame twice.

TIMELINE

1967
Fleetwood Mac form

1974
Fleetwood Mac move to the U.S., adding Stevie Nicks and Lindsey Buckingham

1977
***Rumours* is released, later becoming one of history's best-selling albums**

Notable Members:
Mick Fleetwood, John McVie, Christine McVie, Lindsey Buckingham, Stevie Nicks, Peter Green

Place Formed:
London, England

Dates Active:
1967–2022

Types of Music:
pop rock, blues rock, folk

First Hit Song:
"Albatross" (1968)

A BEST-SELLING ALBUM

Rumours came out in 1977. It won the Grammy for Album of the Year. It is one of history's best-selling albums. *Tango in the Night* came out in 1987. The album scored four *Billboard* Top 20 hits.

ROCK TRAILBLAZERS

Fleetwood Mac took rock in new directions. Members Stevie Nicks and Christine McVie are trailblazers for women in rock.

HIT RELEASES

- *Fleetwood Mac* (1975)
- *Rumours* (1977)
- *Tusk* (1979)
- *Mirage* (1982)
- *Tango in the Night* (1987)

1987
The *Tango in the Night* album earns four *Billboard* Top 20 hits

1998
Fleetwood Mac are added to the Rock & Roll Hall of Fame

QUEEN

Queen changed expectations of what rock stars looked like. They combined hard rock with opera and pop. They were known for their showy stage costumes.

HEAVY METAL BEGINNINGS

Queen formed in 1971. Their early work was heavy metal. In 1974, "Killer Queen" was their first worldwide hit.

Notable Members:
Freddie Mercury, Brian May, John Deacon, Roger Taylor

Place Formed:
London, England

Dates Active:
1971–present

Types of Music:
glam rock, hard rock, arena rock

First Hit Song:
"Seven Seas of Rhye" (1974)

QUEEN

THE GREATEST PERFORMERS

Queen's 1975 song "Bohemian Rhapsody" topped British charts for months. Their 1980 album *The Game* included two Hot 100 chart-toppers. Their performance at the 1985 Live Aid concert is considered one of the greatest ever.

PUSHING BOUNDARIES

Queen pushed musical boundaries to create a new rock sound. They have sold over 300 million albums worldwide.

HIT RELEASES

- ***Sheer Heart Attack*** (1974)
- ***A Night at the Opera*** (1975)
- ***News of the World*** (1977)
- ***Jazz*** (1978)
- ***The Game*** (1980)

TIMELINE

1971
Queen form

1974
"Killer Queen" becomes Queen's first worldwide hit

1975
"Bohemian Rhapsody" is released, soon becoming Queen's signature song

1980
The Game album scores Queen's first two Hot 100 chart-toppers

1985
Queen famously perform at Live Aid

AC/DC

AC/DC are hard rock pioneers. They are known for their high-energy guitar riffs and live performances.

A FAMILY BAND

Sibling guitarists Angus and Malcolm Young formed AC/DC in 1973. They first performed blues rock. "T.N.T." was one of their early hits in 1975.

Notable Members:
Angus Young, Malcolm Young, Bon Scott, Brian Johnson, Phil Rudd, Cliff Williams

Place Formed:
Sydney, Australia

Dates Active:
1973–present

Types of Music:
hard rock, heavy metal, arena rock

First Hit Song:
"T.N.T." (1975)

BACK IN BLACK

AC/DC's 1980 album *Back in Black* sold 50 million copies. It is one of history's best-selling albums. In 1991, "Moneytalks" became their highest-charting *Billboard* song. "War Machine" earned AC/DC their first Grammy for Best Hard Rock Performance in 2010.

POP CULTURE ICONS

AC/DC have inspired countless hard rock artists. Their music continues to play a major role in pop culture today.

BRIAN JOHNSON

HIT RELEASES

Let There Be Rock (1977)

Back in Black (1980)

For Those About to Rock (1981)

The Razors Edge (1990)

Black Ice (2008)

TIMELINE

1973
Brothers Angus and Malcolm Young form AC/DC

1980
The *Back in Black* album releases, eventually becoming one of history's best-selling albums

1991
"Moneytalks" becomes AC/DC's highest-charting song on the *Billboard* Hot 100

2003
AC/DC are added to the Rock & Roll Hall of Fame

2010
"War Machine" earns AC/DC their first Grammy for Best Hard Rock Performance

JOAN JETT

Joan Jett is a trailblazer for women in rock music. She is a skilled guitarist.

THE RUNAWAYS

Jett was first a member of the Runaways. She played guitar and sang vocals. This all-female band formed in 1973. They had hit singles such as "Cherry Bomb."

Birthday:
September 22, 1958

Hometown:
Wynnewood, Pennsylvania

Types of Music:
punk rock, glam rock, heavy metal

First Hit Song:
"Cherry Bomb" (1976)

TIMELINE

1973
Jett joins the Runaways

1980
Jett forms Joan Jett & the Blackhearts

1982
The song "I Love Rock 'N' Roll" reaches number one on the *Billboard* Hot 100 chart

HIT RELEASES

The Runaways (1976)

Bad Reputation (1981)

I Love Rock 'N' Roll (1981)

Good Music (1986)

Up Your Alley (1988)

INSPIRING OTHERS

Jett inspired many other female rock bands, including Bikini Kill, L7, and Babes in Toyland.

JOAN JETT & THE BLACKHEARTS

In the 1980s, Jett formed Joan Jett & the Blackhearts. Their hit albums included *I Love Rock 'N' Roll* and *Good Music*. They were added to the Rock & Roll Hall of Fame in 2015.

1989
Jett is nominated for a Grammy

2015
Joan Jett & the Blackhearts are added to the Rock & Roll Hall of Fame

METALLICA

Metallica are heavy metal icons. They brought the subgenre to new levels of success.

A NEWSPAPER FORMATION

Metallica formed in 1981. The members met after drummer Lars Ulrich placed a newspaper ad. They looked up to artists including Motörhead and Black Sabbath.

MASTERPIECE ALBUMS

Metallica's 1986 album *Master of Puppets* is often called a masterpiece. Their 1991 album *Metallica* sold over 20 million U.S. copies. Its song "Enter Sandman" received worldwide airplay. Metallica earned their ninth Grammy win in 2024 with "72 Seasons."

OPENING NEW DOORS

Metallica opened new doors for heavy metal artists. They were added to the Rock & Roll Hall of Fame in 2009.

Notable Members:
James Hetfield, Lars Ulrich, Kirk Hammett, Jason Newsted, Cliff Burton, Robert Trujillo

Place Formed:
Los Angeles, California

Dates Active:
1981–present

Types of Music:
heavy metal, hard rock

First Hit Song:
"Whiplash" (1983)

HIT RELEASES

Ride the Lightning (1984)

Master of Puppets (1986)

...And Justice for All (1988)

Metallica (1991)

Load (1996)

TIMELINE

1981
Metallica form after their members respond to a newspaper ad

1986
Master of Puppets is released, which critics call a masterpiece

1991
Metallica is released, eventually selling more than 20 million U.S. copies

2009
Metallica are added to the Rock & Roll Hall of Fame

2024
"72 Seasons" earns Metallica their ninth Grammy win

LINKIN PARK

Linkin Park are rock innovators. Their blend of hard rock with hip-hop created a whole new sound.

FOUNDING MEMBERS

Linkin Park formed in 1996. Chester Bennington was the lead singer. Mike Shinoda rapped verses. He also wrote and produced songs.

A BEST-SELLING DEBUT

Their album *Hybrid Theory* came out in 2000. It is the 21st century's best-selling debut album. Its song "In the End" is one of rock's most-streamed songs. The band soon made "Numb/Encore" with Jay-Z. It won the 2006 Grammy for Best Rap/Sung Collaboration.

TIMELINE

1996
Linkin Park form

2000
Hybrid Theory becomes the best-selling debut album of the 21st century

2002
"Crawling" wins the Grammy for Best Hard Rock Performance

A NEW GENERATION

Linkin Park inspired a new generation of rock fans. Their songs have also raised awareness for mental health.

EMILY ARMSTRONG

HIT RELEASES

Hybrid Theory (2000)

Meteora (2003)

Minutes to Midnight (2007)

A Thousand Suns (2010)

Living Things (2012)

Notable Members:
Chester Bennington, Mike Shinoda, Brad Delson, Dave Farrell, Joe Hahn, Rob Bourdon, Emily Armstrong

Place Formed:
Agoura Hills, California

Dates Active:
1996–2017, 2024–present

Types of Music:
hard rock, heavy metal, rap rock

First Hit Song:
"One Step Closer" (2000)

AGOURA HILLS

2006
"Numb/Encore" wins the Grammy for Best Rap/Sung Collaboration

2024
Linkin Park return with a new album seven years after Bennington's death

HAYLEY WILLIAMS

Hayley Williams is the lead singer of Paramore. Her singing and songwriting have made her an icon.

PARAMORE

Paramore formed in 2004. Their 2007 album, *RIOT!*, was their first album to hit the *Billboard* 200 chart. Their 2013 album, *Paramore*, hit number one. Their 2023 album *This Is Why* won two Grammys.

Birthday:
December 27, 1988

Hometown:
Meridian, Mississippi

Types of Music:
alternative rock, indie rock, pop-punk

First Hit Song:
"Misery Business" (2007)

HIT RELEASES

RIOT! (2007)

Paramore (2013)

Petals for Armor (2020)

This Is Why (2023)

Ego Death at a Bachelorette Party (2025)

GOING SOLO

Williams released her first solo album in 2020. It was called *Petals for Armor.* Reviewers praised it. Her 2025 album, *Ego Death at a Bachelorette Party,* was nominated for four Grammys.

GRAMMY WINNER

With Paramore, Williams has won three Grammys. She is praised for her songwriting and bending genres.

PARAMORE

TIMELINE

2004 Williams forms Paramore

2007 *RIOT!* is Paramore's first album to reach the *Billboard* 200 chart

2020 Williams releases her first solo album, *Petals for Armor*

2024 Paramore win two Grammys for *This Is Why*

2026 Williams is nominated for four Grammys

THE FUTURE OF ROCK

Many modern guitars and drum kits are digital. They have sensors that help artists mix and edit music in real time. Virtual reality allows rock stars to give show-stopping performances to fans everywhere.

Imagine Dragons and Olivia Rodrigo rule modern rock charts. Tame Impala and HAIM are top alternative artists. Dominic Fike and Twenty One Pilots keep rap rock popular. WILLOW and Machine Gun Kelly have led a punk rock comeback. Rock has many subgenres. Its fans will surely continue rocking out for many years ahead!

GLOSSARY

airplay—the number of times a song is streamed or played on the radio

alternative—related to something different and typically outside of the mainstream

British Invasion—a cultural phenomenon in the mid 1960s when British rock music became popular in the U.S.

choruses—catchy, repetitive parts of songs that illustrate the song's main message

collaboration—something created while working with others

debut—first appearance

distorted—a changed or edited sound

generations—groups of people who were born around the same time

genre—a category for a type of music

innovators—people who create new ideas and techniques or who positively change existing ones

inspired—gave someone an idea about what to do or create

mainstream—something that is common and shared by a large audience

melodies—series of lyrics and sounds that are arranged with a rhythm

nominated—chosen as a candidate for an award

percussion—instruments that make sound when struck or shaken

performance art—an art form that relies on music, dancing, and fashion to tell a story

pop culture—the trends and art that define a particular society

rhythms—repeated patterns of movement or sound

riffs—short, repeated notes that form the main rhythms of a song

solos—parts of songs where only one instrument is played; artists who work alone are called solo artists.

subgenres—smaller, more specific types of music within a genre

tempo—pace of a song

virtual reality—digital environments that users can visit through technology such as headsets

WRITE ABOUT IT!

- Which artist do you think has had the biggest impact on rock? **Why?**
- What are some of your favorite rock songs? **Why do you like them?**
- How do you think rock music will continue to **change** in the future?

ALSO CHECK OUT

INDEX

The images in this book are reproduced through the courtesy of:
Voloshyn Roman, front cover (hero); Ruslan Lytvyn, front cover
(amp); Ben Houdijk, front cover (drummer), pp. 9 (top), 12 (midd
13 (bottom), 45 (top right); LIGHTFIELD STUDIOS, front cover
(singer); Adam McCullough, pp. 3 (Stevie Nicks), 5 (bottom);
Sven-Sebastian Sajak/ Wikimedia Commons, pp. 3 (Billie Joe
Armstrong), 42 (top right); Doug McKenzie/ Getty Images,
pp. 3 (Jimi Hendrix), 29 (Jimi Hendrix); J.A. Dunbar, p. 4 (top);
Kevin Mazur/ Getty Images, p. 4 (bottom); Pictorial Press/ Alam
Stock Photo, p. 5 (top); Tibrina Hobson/ Getty Images, p. 5
(middle); Pickwick Records/ Wikimedia Commons, p. 6 (top); Br
Yeung, p. 6 (middle); Klaus Hiltscher/ Wikimedia Commons, p. 6
(bottom left); CrowbarCatalyst/ Wikimedia Commons, p. 6 (bott
right); Michael Putland/ Getty Images, pp. 7 (top), 26-27, 30 (to
Tony Norkus, p. 7 (middle left); Richard E. Aaron/ Getty Images,
pp. 7 (middle right), 32 (bottom); Jeffrey Mayer/ Getty Images,
p. 7 (bottom); Tim Mosenfelder/ Getty Images, p. 8 (top); Jeff
Kravitz/ Getty Images, pp. 8 (middle), 18-19; Maj.l, p. 8 (bottor
Raph_PH/ Wikimedia Commons, pp. 9 (middle), 31 (bottom), 4
(bottom left); CyberEak, p. 9 (bottom); wetwebwork/ Wikimedia
Commons, p. 10 (1931); hor RCA/ Wikimedia Commons, p. 10
(1956); Bernd Schwabe/ Wikimedia Commons, pp. 10 (gramm
14 (grammy), 23 (grammy), 35 (grammy), 40 (grammy), 41
(grammy); Mauvries, pp. 10 (1964), 27 (middle); Dezo Hoffmar
Wikimedia Commons, pp. 10-11; Michael Barera/ Wikimedia
Commons, p. 11 (1983); Pete Still/ Getty Images, p. 11 (1985)
Kevin Winter/ Getty Images, p. 11 (2006); lev radin, p. 11
(2026); irish10567/ Wikimedia Commons, p. 12 (top); Museum
of Making Music/ Wikimedia Commons, p. 12 (bottom left); Pav
L Photo and Video, p. 12 (bottom right); Dominionart, p. 13 (top)
Frazer Harrison/ Getty Images, pp. 14-15; SUSAN GOLDMAN
Getty Images, p. 15 (top left); Featureflash Photo Agency, p. 15
(top right); Kathy Hutchins, p. 15 (middle); Emma McIntyre/ Get
Images, pp. 15 (Rock & Roll Hall of Fame), 21 (Rock & Roll Hall
of Fame), 27 (Rock & Roll Hall of Fame), 29 (Rock & Roll Hall
of Fame), 31 (Rock & Roll Hall of Fame), 35 (Rock & Roll Hall
of Fame), 37 (Rock & Roll Hall of Fame); Vinnie Zuffante/ Getty
Images, p. 15 (bottom right); FilmPublicity/ Getty Images, p. 16
(left); Gems/ Redferns/ Getty Images, pp. 16 (right), 34 (top);
Pete Still/ Redferns/ Getty Images, p. 17 (left); Paul Natkin/ Get
Images, pp. 17 (right), 21 (bottom); Chris Walter/ Getty Images
p. 18 (left); David Redfern/ Getty Images, pp. 19 (top), 20-21,
24 (top), 29 (bottom left); FashionStock.com, p. 19 (bottom); Joo
van Bilsen/ Wikipedia, p. 20 (top); Brian Rasic/ Getty Images,
p. 20 (middle); Michael Ochs Archives/ Getty Images, pp. 20
(bottom left), 22 (middle left), 24 (bottom left), 30 (bottom), 34
(middle top); Kovacs, p. 20 (bottom right); NBC Television/
Wikimedia Commons, p. 21 (top); NASA/ JPL/ Wikipedia, p. 2
(middle); http://www.classic-motorcycle-build.com/ Wikimedia
Commons, p. 22 (top left); Mr. Littlehand/ Wikipedia Commons,
p. 22 (top middle); Edward Roth/ Wikimedia Commons, p. 22
(top right); Fredlyfish4/ Wikimedia Commons, p. 22 (middle righ
Batfan1966/ Wikipedia Commons, p. 22 (bottom);
Metro-Goldwyn-Mayer, Inc./ Wikimedia Commons, p. 23 (top);
Sunset Boulevard/ Getty Images, p. 23 (middle); Fallaner/
Wikimedia Commons, p. 23 (bottom); Michael Cooper/ Wikime
Commons, p. 24 (middle); Aerial Film Studio, p. 24 (bottom
right); Daily Mirror/ Getty Images, pp. 24-25; Associated Press/
Wikimedia Commons, p. 25 (top); Universal Archive/ Getty Ima
p. 27 (top left); Leonid Andronov, p. 27 (top right); Jim Pietryga/
Wikimedia Commons, p. 27 (bottom); Scanpix/ Wikimedia
Commons, p. 28 (top); Blick/ RDB/ ullstein bild/ Getty Images,
p. 28 (middle); Marjut Valakivi/ Wikimedia Commons, pp. 28
(bottom left), 29 (middle); Claude Humbert/ Wikimedia Commo
p. 28 (bottom right); Diegomezr, p. 29 (bottom right); s4svisuals,
p. 31 (top); Dia Dipasupil/ Getty Images, p. 31 (middle); Mark
and Colleen Hayward/ Getty Images, pp. 32-33; Alfeeee, p. 32
(middle); Richard Creamer/ Getty Images, p. 33 (middle); David
Tan/ Shinko/ Getty Images, p. 33 (bottom); Alan Smithers,
p. 34 (middle bottom); Fin Costello/ Getty Images, pp. 34 (botto
left), 38 (bottom); Photography Stock Ruiz, p. 34 (bottom right),
35 (middle); Watal Asanuma/ Getty Images, p. 35 (bottom); Ai
Lehtonen, p. 36 (top left); David Johnson/ Wikimedia Commons,
p. 36 (top middle); Randy Miramontez, p. 36 (top right); Joe See
p. 36 (bottom left); Ii2nmd/ Wikimedia Commons, p. 36 (bottom
right); Daniel L. Locke, p. 37; Newport Coast Media, p. 38 (top)
Achim Raschka/ Wikimedia Commons, p. 38 (middle); Library o
Congress Life/ Wikimedia Commons, pp. 38-39; Ross Marino/
Getty Images, p. 39 (top); ANP/ Getty Images, p. 40 (top);
s_bukley, pp. 40-41; mooinblack, p. 40 (bottom); Sergione Infus
Getty Images, p. 41 (top); James Minchin III/ Wikimedia Comm
p. 41 (bottom left); Matt Gush, p. 41 (bottom right); Ralph PH/
Wikimedia Commons, p. 42 (top left); Sabrina Janelle Gordon,
p. 42 (middle); Debby Wong, p. 42 (bottom left); phillyist/
Wikimedia Commons, p. 42 (bottom right); yakub88, p. 43 (top
L Paul Mann, pp. 43 (bottom), 45 (middle left); WHYFRAME, p.
(top); Adam Gasson/ Alamy Stock Photo, p. 44 (middle); ROBY
BECK/ Getty Images, p. 44 (bottom left); Best smile studio, p. 44
(bottom right); Christian Bertrand, p. 45 (top); Paras Griffin/ Get
Images, p. 45 (middle right); Brandon